Renfermant des scènes stupéfiantes d'illusionnisme naturaliste, le luxueux livre de prières intitulé *Heures de Spinola* est l'un des manuscrits flamands les plus sophistiqués du XVIème siècle sur le plan visuel.

Un livre d'heures contient notamment un calendrier des fêtes religieuses, les Heures de la Vierge (un cycle de prières consacrées à la Vierge Marie), l'Office des morts, et d'autres prières, hymnes et lectures. Dans cet exemplaire, le contenu traditionnel est complété par une série spéciale d'offices et de messes en semaine, ce qui élargit le champ des possibles pour créer de magnifiques enluminures. Le livre a sans doute été commandé pour un riche mécène, peut-être Marguerite d'Autriche, pour qui le Maître de Jacques IV d'Écosse, un célèbre peintre et enlumineur de manuscrits, a produit d'autres œuvres. Dans les années 1700, il appartenait à la famille Spinola de Gênes, dont il tire son nom contemporain.

Nous sommes honorés de présenter cet exemple inégalé d'enluminure conservée au J. Paul Getty Museum dans le cadre de notre collection collaborative.

Das prächtige *Spinola-Stundenbuch* gilt mit seinen verblüffenden naturalistischen Illustrationen als eines der visuell wohl raffiniertesten flämischen Manuskripte des 16. Jahrhunderts.

Das Gebetbuch enthält verschiedene Texte wie einen Kirchenfeiertagskalender, die *Stunden der Jungfrau* (Andachtszyklus zu Ehren von Jungfrau Maria) sowie Gebete, Hymnen und Lektüren. Diese spezielle Ausgabe wurde durch besondere Wochentagsoffizien und -messen ergänzt, was zusätzliche Möglichkeiten zur prächtigen Illustration bot. Das Buch wurde ohne Zweifel von einer Patronin bzw. einem Patron in Auftrag gegeben, möglicherweise von Margarete von Österreich, für welche bereits der Meister von Jakob IV von Schottland, ein berühmter Manuskriptillustrator und Maler, Arbeiten geschaffen hatte. Im 18. Jahrhundert war es in Besitz der Spinola-Familie in Genua, die ihm seinen heutigen Namen gab.

Wir freuen uns, dieses einmalige Illustrationsexemplar aus dem J. Paul Getty Museum in unserer Kollektion zu präsentieren.

Il lussuoso libro di preghiere noto come *Libro d'Ore Spinola*, con pagine che mostrano stupefacenti miniature ispirate alla natura, è uno dei manoscritti fiamminghi più ricercati del XVI secolo.

Un libro d'ore contiene testi come il calendario delle festività della Chiesa, preghiere dedicate alla Vergine Maria, l'ufficio dei defunti e altre preghiere, inni e letture. Questo particolare esemplare è arricchito con una serie speciale di uffici e messe dei giorni feriali, e pertanto di un maggior numero di raffinate miniature. Il libro fu probabilmente commissionato da Margherita d'Austria, per la quale il Maestro di Giacomo IV di Scozia, famoso miniatore e pittore, produsse altre opere. Nel Settecento apparteneva alla famiglia Spinola di Genova, da cui prende il nome attuale.

Siamo onorati di introdurre nella nostra collezione questo incomparabile esempio di testo miniato conservato presso il J. Paul Getty Museum.

El suntuoso libro de oraciones personal conocido como el *Libro de horas de Spínola*, cuyas páginas albergan asombrosas muestras de ilusionismo naturalista, es uno de los manuscritos iluminados flamencos más sofisticados del siglo XVI.

Los libros de horas incluyen varios textos, como un calendario de festividades religiosas, las horas de la Virgen (un ciclo de plegarias dedicadas a la Virgen María), el oficio de difuntos y otras oraciones, himnos y lecturas. Este ejemplo en concreto amplía el contenido con una serie especial de oficios y misas de diario, lo que da pie a una mayor profusión de iluminaciones. No hay duda de que el libro se encargó para una acaudalada mecenas, quizá Margarita de Austria, para quien el Maestro de Jacobo IV de Escocia, afamado pintor e iluminador de manuscritos, realizó otras obras. En el siglo XVIII perteneció a la familia Spínola de Génova, de la que toma su nombre actual.

Es un honor presentar este incomparable ejemplar de manuscrito iluminado conservado en el J. Paul Getty Museum como parte de nuestra colección colaborativa.

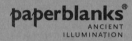

paperblanks®
ANCIENT
ILLUMINATION

Spinola Hours

With pages displaying astounding plays of naturalistic illusionism, the luxurious personal prayer book known as the *Spinola Hours* is one of the most visually sophisticated Flemish manuscripts of the 16th century.

A book of hours contains texts including a calendar of Church holidays, the Hours of the Virgin (a cycle of prayer services devoted to the Virgin Mary), the Office for the Dead, and other prayers, hymns and readings. This particular example augments these contents with a special series of weekday offices and masses, providing even more possibilities for rich illuminations. The book was undoubtedly commissioned for a wealthy patron, perhaps Margaret of Austria, for whom the Master of James IV of Scotland, a famed manuscript illuminator and painter, produced other works. In the 1700s it belonged to the Spinola family in Genoa, from whom it takes its modern name.

We are honoured to feature this unparalleled example of illumination from the J. Paul Getty Museum as part of our collaborative collection.

ISBN: 978-1-4397-9391-6
ULTRA FORMAT   176 PAGES   LINED
DESIGNED IN CANADA

Getty